ANTON DOMNEY

SMOKING AND SOLUTIONS

**The Ultimate Guide to Crushing the Smoking Habit,
Discover Effective Strategies and Tips on How to Break the
Habit and Stop Smoking Permanently**

Descrierea CIP a Bibliotecii Naţionale a României
ANTON DOMNEY
   SMOKING AND SOLUTIONS. The Ultimate Guide to
Crushing the Smoking Habit, Discover Effective Strategies and
Tips on How to Break the Habit and Stop Smoking Permanently /
Anton Domney – Bucharest: Editura My Ebook, 2021
   ISBN

ANTON DOMNEY

SMOKING AND SOLUTIONS

**The Ultimate Guide to Crushing the Smoking Habit,
Discover Effective Strategies and Tips on How to Break the
Habit and Stop Smoking Permanently**

My Ebook Publishing House
Bucharest, 2021

TABLE OF CONTENTS

Understanding the Psychology of Smoking

A couple of years back, everyone thought it was cool to smoke in public. Some people even implied that smoking helped you get an edge on your peers by giving you an air of confidence when puffing away. With a cigarette you were the one everyone wanted to be like in your circle of friends. It was believed that the opposite sex was supposedly more attracted to you, if you were fashionably smoking away. Smoking is believed by some to make the man more virile.

Even though you might wonder why everything that is perceived as cool is linked with virility, let's focus on this whole cigarette business and how it has practically brought mankind to its knees. A globally conducted survey statistically reveals facts about smoking and its harmful effects on the body. The study compared the impact of the damage causing deaths to smokers like the destruction of those who died in the Hiroshima and Nagasaki bombings in Japan.

Right now, scientists label smoking as the largest preventable cause of premature diseases and early death. Every minute, one in fifteen adults is dying of lung cancer. This is attributed to the addictive nature of smoking, resulting in an annual four million deaths (this is an approximate figure). Tobacco usage pertains to not only smoking, but also chewing betel leaves and inhaling deadly snuff. But still in spite of these facts it is worth noticing that approximately 15 billion cigarettes are sold daily. That is a HUGE figure! Who smokes that much and WHY?

About one in three cigarettes consumed is in the Western Pacific Region of the world. The tobacco market is controlled by just a few corporations - namely American, British and Japanese multinational conglomerates. Among young teens (aged 13 - 15), about one in five smokes throughout the world. They indulge in this cruel habit known as "fagging" despite being aware of the fact that cigarette smoke contains more than four thousand carcinogenic substances.

When a smoker smokes in the presence of non smokers, he is affecting them with toxic substances, perhaps more than himself. It has been proven scientifically that passive smoking has been found to be the worst and most unpredictable cause of massive illnesses on various populations.

Approximately 80,000 to 100,000 children start smoking every day. These figures include both adolescents and teenagers. There is a tendency for those who start to smoke at a young age to not be able to quit in their adulthoods. What pushes these teenagers to mindlessly follow a fad which later goes on to become one of their life's biggest problems? Perhaps it's the glamorous advertisements of cigarettes, where the smoker is shown to be the alpha male. Where the "real man" is capable of achieving the most impossible of feats against the most improbable of odds because he smokes. If it's not that it just may be their favorite movie stars lighting up in style, just before an intense moment of action or a power play. What teen wouldn't want to imitate that image? Researchers concluded that all the afore mentioned factors definitely arouses a person's desire to smoke. However, if we really need to get to the bottom of this mystery, we must start at the very roots of the problem. We need to take time out to understand the psychology of smoking and why it's so hard to give up the addicting habit.

Whenever scientists start analyzing any problem, they first look for the symptoms of the disease. It is safe to say the smoking is a disease of addiction. If you have been addicted to cigarettes for an adequate part of your life, you would have noticed that the hardest part of quitting is to beat the cravings. A heavily dependent smoker wants just one more cigarette almost every other instant of his waking hours. Even in his sleep he has smoke-hazy dreams of enjoying exotic versions of cigarettes. Addicts report that after a point of time, the smoking habit takes over so badly and unconsciously that one starts smoking irrespective of where he is, or what he is doing. After a day of hard work, in order to relax a person might feel like smoking till he gets decidedly sleepy. It is nicotine, the active and the most harmful neurotransmitter present in tobacco that successfully numbs his senses.

Knopfler might have glorified the fact that rock stars have nicotine for breakfast, but Angus rightfully said that 'smoking turns one too old to rock and roll but too young to die!' How is it that nicotine successfully takes over the human mind and makes us lose control of our bodies and lives?

Acetylcholine is one of the most important neuro-transmitters present in the body. Acetylcholine nerve receptors at the synapses resemble those of nicotine.

Nicotine rushes to the pain receptors and other sense receptors and blocks these sites cutting short the normal passage of nervous impulse. This causes the blockage of information essential for the central nervous system to function so as the result transmitters keep on trying to reach the necessary pathways. It just so happens that with every additional cigarette the effect gets more and more pronounced. Once you are done with your first puff, the sensation of numbness wears off fast and in order to prolong the fuzzy feeling, you unconsciously reach out for another cigarette. This is one of the primary symptoms of nicotine induced withdrawals, something which is the very germ of the whole smoking catastrophe. Remember that every cigarette smoked cuts out at least five minutes of your normal life span. Is that a happy thought? Think about it!

Every cigarette manufacturer provides the disclaimer on their pack of cigarettes that "Cigarette smoking is injurious to health." Now this might seem like a hoax, almost a challenge to your immune system, but the Physician General who writes the disclaimer does so because he has seen the far reaching consequences of nicotine, like lung cancer and premature death.

Have you heard of the Pavlovian study? The famous Russian biologist found that he can make a dog salivate during its eating time without actually serving him food. He did so by ringing a bell which set off an impulse of craving in its nervous system. Similarly in a smoker, it is found that if they are accustomed to smoking in presence of a cup of coffee or in the company of friends, their body is conditioned to wanting to smoke near such stimuli.

Are You Addicted To Smoking? The Smokers Quiz

How on earth did you get addicted to smoking? You may have been wondering this for a while without having any clue about it. Through this chapter, we will try to help you determine whether you're actually addicted to smoking or not.

Remember the first time you smoked?

Most people tell a similar story about their first cigarette. It goes like this: You were hanging out with a few friends, one of them handed you a cigarette and asked you to see how it felt to take a drag. You tried to inhale it, coughed over it and there....that was your first smoke.

Why did you continue anyway? Like the others, did you find the habit of smoking to be a stress remover? Did you think you can depend on smoking to take your worries and the fatigue away? Does it soothe you, and make you happy?

One way or another, cigarettes have turned out to be the cool way out, especially among youngsters. Your body might hate it, but your mind is always propelling you to go on lest you start missing out on something.

Of course once you are all into it, smoking is like a crutch that you need so you can continue walking in your life. You spend loads of money on it; you limit your lifespan and yet you go on and on. You think it's the elusive supplement to life that keeps you going. Don't be mad about your excuses because these are the same reasons that thousands of other smokers use too.

You may have tried to quit, but it is really not as easy as you thought. You may be worried about the withdrawal symptoms that you might have to deal with, amongst other things. Somehow the whole proposition of quitting smoking seems a little too unrealistic for you.

Here, as we let you evaluate your addiction and the possible characteristics associated with it, let me tell you, it is not about simply answering a few questions. It is also about letting you judge for yourself what the problems are and how much your dependence on cigarettes is.

It is up to you now to decide whether you want to wriggle free of the habit or just succumb to your addiction and let it continue to control your life.

Take a look at these questions:

1. Do you smoke daily? If so for how long have you been smoking daily?

2. Check the following list and answer honestly to yourself, which of these do you experience after you stop or cut down on the amount of smoking. These symptoms can set in immediately after you have taken a break from smoking.

- ❑ Anxiety
- ❑ Decrease in heart rate
- ❑ Depression and mood swings
- ❑ Difficulty in concentrating
- ❑ Increased appetite or weight gain
- ❑ Insomnia
- ❑ Restlessness
- ❑ Unexplainable irritability, frustration or anger

3. How badly do the symptoms mentioned above set in when you experience them? Do you have to postpone all work because of them?

Check if the answer to all or most of the symptoms above is yes. In case it is a yes, it's time for you to get some help. Try not to procrastinate at this point because you are starting to see that your addiction is worse than you initially thought. Instead of being in denial; save that energy to gather up all the courage you need to take on this problem head-on.

4. Can you remember a single day in the last year or so when you did not smoke at all?

If you can remember a day in your life where you did not smoke then, try and remember how you managed to stay free of smoking that day. Try and re-enact the same things you did that day that kept you from smoking. If you can't remember not smoking, then don't worry, you're not the only one. It doesn't mean you should give up all together on quitting. It's just means you need to put more effort into your next attempt. It's not the end of the world, just add a little patience and strength of mind to the equation and before you know it you will be free of cigarettes for good.

5. Do you smoke in spite of having a condition related to tobacco addiction like bronchitis or COPD (Chronic Obstructive Pulmonary Disease)?

If you are experiencing any illnesses related to smoking, then remember that most smokers do have a sense of the medical problems that they face from their habit. A lung condition, a heart condition, a mouth condition, or general side effects does not stop the addicted smoker. Nothing deters them because they are

15

addicted to the nicotine despite the negative health effects that they may be experiencing while they continue to smoke.

6. Is the pleasure or satisfaction from smoking becoming less every day?

Smokers tend to find that in order to get the same feeling that they used to get from their cigarettes when they began smoking, that they need more and more to compensate for that feeling.

7. Do you smoke as much every day in spite of answering yes to the above question?

Because of the recent media exposure a lot of smokers are getting a wakeup call. The threats of cancer and diseases are quite real yet the addict knows this but simply can't stop. If you continue to smoke, despite being aware of all its negative effects then it is obvious that you have a problem. Why else would you willingly subject your body to poison?

8. Are you still a big fan of cigarettes despite knowing of all the negative health effects?

If you said yes, then go over the facts about smoking in your head once again. It kills in the end. It slows down your reflexes and you are literally poisoning your body. It does not do you any good.

It is merely in your head and has a control over you. You are not addicted by choice. Your mind and body both crave nicotine, but the addiction is not impossible to break. It's like you are under a spell. You want to quit but you feel compelled to have one more cigarette. It may sound redundant, but the more you internalize these statements, the faster you are to break free.

9. Have you been anxious or nervous for the first two weeks of quitting smoking whenever you have tried?

If yes, then it is clear that these are part of your withdrawal symptoms. Don't worry. This doesn't mean that you don't have it in you to quit smoking. It merely means that you have to inspire yourself a little more. You have to fight a little harder with your mind. You need a little more strength to continue and we will help you build up the inner strength to overcome the habit.

10. Have you been depressed for the first two weeks after you have tried to quit smoking?

If your answer is yes, then once again we repeat, it is not the biggest obstacle. Again you need to call on your inner strength. Work on your confidence in your decision to quit and make it through one hour at a time. Remember the mantra- "It is not difficult to quit." You just have to deal with it in your head.

Why You Should Quit Smoking Today

Getting rid of a smoking habit is not easy. As a matter of fact, any addiction may initially prove to be immensely tough to get rid of, especially in the case of cigarettes. Trying to quit smoking has specific symptoms that arise due to withdrawing from the habit, and these symptoms make the process seem much more difficult.

From the addiction perspective, nicotine is quite similar to heroin or even cocaine. The effects of the material released into your bloodstream after inhalation is of course less pronounced in the case of nicotine, but it's still as addicting as heroin and cocaine. Smoking brings along with it several diseases, and is definitely a risky and potentially harmful habit which should be left as soon as possible.

Basically, during smoking, a lot of substances which are harmful to us are released inside our body. These substances damage our vital organs like our heart, stomach, liver, lungs and

18

brain. The substances which are toxic reduce the amount of oxygen though out the body causing the immune system to be badly affected. A weakened immune system makes it probable for diseases to develop easier.

The two most common diseases that happen due to smoking are lung cancer and heart complications. It is unfortunate that the majority of smokers at some point in their lives suffer from one or both of these. When we smoke, nicotine resides in the cells of our body. As a result the liver and kidneys have trouble metabolizing the toxic residue which builds up instead of being eliminated.

Therefore even after, say, 12 hours after a person has last smoked, high levels of nicotine can still be found in the smoker's body.

No one said kicking the smoking habit is easy, but there are certain drugs that help in the process: Nicorette patches and gum are a popular example. Chantix is also well known. Chantix is a heavily addictive antidepressant which has some serious and harmful side effects to boot, but is used under the supervision of a doctor for some relief from depression and anxiety related to withdrawal. Later in this e Book, we will talk about various ways that can help you to stop smoking using the various aids that are available. Some aids are over the counter and others require a doctor.

A very long time ago, when our parents were young, smoking was permitted in almost all public places, hospitals included. Cigarettes were majorly advertised. Today things are different. Public awareness has increased in relation to the dangers of smoking thanks to vigilante campaigns and advertisements informing us about the ill effects of smoking to general health. Smoking advertisements are not permitted any longer on TV, radio or magazines, and smoking itself is banned in most public places now to deter the smoker from lighting up.

It's a little surprising when you consider what smoking costs and how people are still willing to continue. Smoking leads to cancer, heart complications and emphysema. It cuts out 10 or more years from the smoker's life and costs him above 4000+ dollars per year to maintain the addiction. But smokers still continue to smoke, because of the addiction.

Quit smoking now! Here's why **not** to continue the habit:

1. Tobacco smoke contains extremely harmful chemicals:

Smoking is harmful. It affects everyone (smokers and nonsmokers alike) who inhales the noxious chemicals in tobacco smoke. Even a little tobacco smoke can be harmful as it contains over 4,000 chemicals, at least 250 of which are known to be particularly dangerous. The toxic chemicals found in smoke include carbon monoxide (found in car exhaust), hydrogen cyanide (used in the manufacture of chemical weapons), formaldehyde (used as an embalming fluid), toluene (found in paint thinners) and ammonia (used in household cleaners).

Of the countless other harmful chemicals in tobacco smoke, more than 50 are proven to be carcinogenic. These include:

o vinyl chloride (toxic substance used in manufacturing plastics)

o polonium-210 (chemical element giving off radiation)

o nickel (harmful metallic element)

o ethylene oxide (chemical used in sterilizing medical devices)

o chromium (harmful metallic element)

o cadmium (metal used in manufacture of batteries)

o beryllium (toxic metal)

o benzene (chemical found in gasoline)

o arsenic (heavy metal toxin leading to poisoning)

2. Smoking causes countless health problems:

Millions of Americans suffer from health problems resulting from cigarette smoking and exposure to tobacco

21

smoke. Together, these cause around 438,000 (estimated average) premature deaths per year in the United States **alone**. Of these premature deaths, around 25 percent result from lung disease, 35 percent from heart disease and stroke, and 40 percent from cancer. Smoking is the leading cause of premature, preventable death in this country.

Harmful for nearly every organ of the body, smoking reduces your overall health and immunity. It is one of the primary causes of cancer, and may result in cancers of the lung, larynx (voice box), mouth, esophagus, throat, pancreas, stomach, kidney, bladder, and cervix, as well as acute myeloid leukemia, often leading to death.

It can also cause lung disease (chronic bronchitis and emphysema), strokes, heart disease, hip fractures, and cataracts. Smokers also lose their immunity and are at higher risk of developing pneumonia and other airway infections. They also risk harming others around them. Women who smoke when pregnant risk having premature delivery and may have babies with abnormally low weight. In addition, smoking during pregnancy and/or breastfeeding is shown to increase the infant's risk of death from Sudden Infant Death Syndrome (SIDS).

Smoking and its ill effects

The human body has no need for tobacco. It is not an essential factor like food, or water. Nicotine and cyanide, chemicals found in the cigarettes, are actually lethal if consumed heavily or inhaled through smoke.

People who try out smoking for the first time find it difficult and many times don't enjoy it for the first time. This is because our body goes in defense mode, sensing the presence of poisons in it. Therefore, those people who smoke for the first time find a burning sensation in the throat and lungs and some even vomit or become sick when they consume tobacco.

Over a period of time however, the body's defenses start breaking down and pave the way for diseases and illnesses like heart complications, strokes, and emphysema (which is nothing but lung tissue breakdown). Cancer is always a possibility; cancer can happen in the lungs, throat, stomach and bladder.

Bronchitis and pneumonia are two infections that can also occur.

These diseases reduce the person's will to be active and energetic – let's not forget they also prove to be fatal as well. Every time you smoke, you cut short 5- 20 minutes of your lifespan. With a pack a day, a smoker can lose up to 6 hours of life per day. That is about $1/4^{th}$ of your life. The average person sleeps for $1/3^{rd}$ of their life so the combined effect of inactivity plus smoking can lead you to losing more than 50% of your productive hours.

Apart from becoming less active and energetic due to the affect smoking has on the bodies lung capacity for air; smoking gives rise to wrinkles and yellow teeth. It reduces bone density causing osteoporosis (**ahs**-tee-o-puh-**row**-sus).

Osteoporosis leads to older men and women becoming bent over and their bones become more fragile and easily breakable.

The consequences of smoking may seem very far off, but long-term health problems aren't the only hazard of smoking. Nicotine and the other toxins in cigarettes, cigars, and pipes can affect a person's body quickly, which means that teen smokers experience many of these health problems due to smoking as well.

Many people think that smoking can only prove to be harmful after a long time, but this is not true at all. Certain effects are immediate and chemicals like nicotine and several other similar toxins can seriously affect a person in several ways at once, without needing any lapse of time. Here are the ways:

❏ Skin problems are caused because of oxygen and required nutrients not reaching the skin. This is because smoking affects blood vessels and restricts them. A skin rash called psoriasis has also been connected with smoking by a report published in Italy. Smokers thus often look very pale and not very healthy.

❏ Halitosis, or continued bad breath is another condition which smokers have.

❏ The smell of smoke is strong and isn't gotten rid of easily. This smell sticks to clothes, hair, cars and furniture.

❏ Athletes should stay away from smoking at all costs because smoking reduces athletic performance by several ways: It increases heartbeat, decreases blood flow in several parts of the body, and leads to shortness of breath.

❏ Smoking leads to less production of collagen and thus increases the risk of injuries. Injuries related to sports generally take longer to heal so it's uncommon for serious athletes to smoke. Smokers also find that tendons, ligaments and muscles take a longer time to heal and to feel "good" again.

❑ Smokers are more susceptible to diseases and illnesses like colds, flu, bronchitis and pneumonia. For asthmatic people, smoking is immensely dangerous, as it is for sick people in general. Smoking inhibits appetite and many teenagers who smoke don't eat properly. Because of lack of appetite they are in loss of essential nutrients they need to help grow and fight ailments.

Smoking and Heart Disease - The Connection

Nicotine in tobacco increases blood pressure greatly and pushes the heart to dangerous limits. Carbon monoxide enters the bloodstream and takes the place of oxygen. Smoking also blocks the arteries which may further lead to heart conditions and complications. Coronary heart diseases are also very prevalent among smokers. All of this should be reason enough for you to want to quit smoking.

Smoking cigarettes, according to medical studies, leads to a higher metabolism rate and loss of appetite. However, whether it is actually loss of appetite or the taste buds losing their ability of taste is heavily debated. The latter may very well be the reason for loss of appetite. Right after people stop smoking, they tend to gain weight. This could be because their taste buds regain their ability to taste which makes meals a lot more enjoyable for the person who doesn't smoke.

Smoking becomes a tough nut to crack over a period of time for a person because of the heavy addiction it causes. Nicotine addiction is very hard to beat; and one of the reasons is that the chemicals that reach the brain from smoking activates the pleasure spots in the brain. This affects the smoker's mood and leads to short term feel-good sensations.

Smoking Affects Sexual Life Too!

The feel good sensation distracts the smoker from the fact that smoking leads to fatal diseases like cancer, emphysema and heart diseases. Even the sexual life of males and females, alike, are affected from smoking. In men erections can be difficult to attain and maintain. This happens due to several reasons, the primary being the role of carbon monoxide. When Carbon monoxide enters the circulatory system, it affects it by hindering blood flow to the penis. This is, as you know, required to get an erection. Smoking has been identified to be one of the primary reasons behind erectile dysfunction.

The Journal of Urology in 2000 released a report which stated that around 68% of men with high blood pressure, around the age of 49-70 suffered from erectile dysfunction. Among these, 45% included serious sexual illnesses linked to smoking. High blood pressure is directly connected to low testosterone.

Testosterone is a male hormone which plays an immensely important part in sexual arousal. It also leads to low sexual performance. Among other harmful effects, toxins in the cigarettes may lead to damaging the testes. Smoking may affect semen and sperm count. The mobility and quality of sperm may deteriorate. Smokers, thus, tend to have a low sperm count and low quality sperms which aren't well formed, compared to non smokers.

In the case of women smokers, smoking may actually harm the ovaries. It is also difficult for women to conceive when they smoke and chances of conceiving are reduced by almost 40%, during each menstrual cycle. So basically, the more a woman smokes the less chance she has of becoming pregnant. Smoking thus wreaks havoc on sexual lives of women too. It affects peoples' sex lives by reducing the quality of sex dramatically in both sexes who smoke. This is another reason for people to want to quit smoking.

There are many programs now available to the public which help people get rid of this habit. One may also contact their personal doctor to learn more about the correct medications which can help them get rid of this terrible addiction once and for all. These medications typically wean the smoker off smoking slowly and get rid of the need to smoke thru a period of time eventually for good. It is a tough process, but if you're concerned about your health, as well as your quitting smoking is the best thing to do.

Quit Smoking Today!

Kicking the butt is considered one of the toughest mental gymnastics one has to do in their lifetime. Cigarettes are addictive because of the harmful nicotine spewing element it contains. Even if someone manages to stay away from the packet of his favorite cigs once in a while; nicotine withdrawal symptoms start to kick in. It is the withdrawal symptoms that make it very difficult for you to resist the temptation of savoring one more puff. Nevertheless, scientists have been delving deeper into the biological effects of smoking and have isolated a range of psychological as well as physiological characteristics which are responsible for making us leech on to this harmful substance. Quite surprisingly, they have come to the conclusion that by reversing the factors concerned they might just be able to weed out this habit from a nicotine addict.

Admitting your addiction to smoking

There is this common tendency among most smokers to be in denial about their smoking attachment. They console themselves by believing they can easily quit the habit of smoking even if they know quite well that in reality they can't. If one finally musters the courage to admit his or her addiction to smoking, he or she is one step closer to beating the smoking addiction. Once this realization sets in, half the battle is won.

Are you a smoker? Are you then ashamed to be seen as some sort of weak person who can never do away with his regular habit of smoking? You have these silly excuses like, "I need something to soothe my nerves" or "It helps me think better". Reasons like "I need to unwind" are also used to defend the habit. Even though smoking is addictive, it's important to not make excuses for your habit. Accept that you have a problem, that's the 1st step in moving forward. Making excuses reinforces that fact that you are incapable of letting go of your habit to begin with, and that you can't do any routine activities without a cigarette. Admit that you are simply addicted to smoking and take the bull by the horns.

This realization is not at all an embarrassment, nor something to feel inferior about. Be bold and proud to stand out from rest of the smoke-addicts. Tobacco is so dangerous that it won't spare you until you succumb terminally. Being caught up in having to smoke causes you to never know when you have finally let its deadly grip over you. It may be too late as it starts contaminating each breath you take. You and only you can save yourself.

The first thing I suggest for you to do is to take a look at yourself in the mirror. Look at your image at least for a minute. Try to visualize the cigarette and its smoke as a bunch of tentacles of a deadly octopus that has already gripped you from all around. It is perhaps at this crucial moment that the realization would dawn upon you that you are in fact addicted to smoking.

The thought might appear infuriating initially; humiliating on the first take. It may hurt your pride. But I tell you this is not the time to lose control of yourself. It

takes a strong person to accept their weaknesses. Don't look upon it as something damaging to your ego, rather muster the courage to face it. Only then will you be able to fight back and regain your self-esteem.

You must take heed that this is no ordinary battle that we are talking about. It's a hard battle that you have to fight until you win. In fact if you stick to the fight eventually *you **will*** win.

Smoking will only beat you if you let it beat you. You are the one that lights the cigarette; no one is putting a gun to your head. This manual will show you different methods you can use to end your addiction, but ultimately you have to stick to the game plan to end to be victorious. We can give you a map to success, but you are the one that has to follow its directions.

All cigarettes are equally bad

Of course the more cigarettes you smoke the more harm you invite for yourself. Knowing this would make you extremely foolish on your part not to recognize the impact of the harm even a single puff can cause you. Smoking any number of cigarettes is actually harmful; although the degree of harm goes up with each increasing number of cigarettes.

Your smoking addiction does not care about the characteristic features of a particular cigarette. It cares only about getting the nicotine that your body craves. Irrespective of whether it comes from a filtered or a menthol cigarette, whether you smoke less frequently or more the long term results are the same. Smoking decays your lungs first and then every other part of your body with each toxic smoke you inhale.

Mentally Prepare Yourself to Quit Smoking

There are a lot of instances in life when one has serious doubts of what he is capable of. A common phenomenon is when a smoker willing to quit his habit feels that he is a victim of his circumstances and that causes him stress. Finding a successful way of quitting smoking is a tough job but if you can find a formula for quitting that works for you, then you are very likely to be successful. It is very important to imagine that you have successfully quit smoking before you even start. If you develop that vision, then it will be easier for you to accomplish your goal.

It is very important for you to understand that how you perceive yourself and how you think has an extremely significant impact on your odds of quitting. Many times smoking is just a manifestation of other problems one has. The unseen under lying reasons which compel a person to smoke have to also be addressed to help the smoker in his recovery. Some of these issues may be and include:

> Relief from stress
> Getting rid of boredom
> Trying to fit into an image
> Trying to imitate the group he belongs to
> Loss of weight
> Addiction

So prior to planning to quit smoking, it is important that you analyze the reasons which compelled you to turn to smoking. You can replace smoking with other healthier substitutes to take care of your root problem. In such a case, you will not succumb to the temptation of smoking in that particular situation. Since each person is unique, it is essential that everyone develops his own ways of quitting smoking. For example, my father who was an avid smoker would take a piece of candy every time he felt the urge to smoke. Although modern medicine makes the coping of nicotine withdrawal easier, my point is you need to find a substitute or outlet during the duration of your recovery process.

There is another preparation which you can make mentally. Stop seeing cigarettes as a source of pleasure, but as something you wish to get rid of. Every time you get an urge to smoke remind yourself that every additional puff you take is a minute of your life you will never get back. You need to be strong and realize smoking not only affects your life, but it affects the life of all those around you.

Another good thing to do is to make a list of all bad things which will not happen to you if you quit smoking. Also remind yourself of the positive effects of a non- smoking life. Fighting the habit is hard, but keeping a daily "reference sheet" or hanging up signs around your house will help you stay focused. One of the reasons why people go back to smoking is that they end up saying "this will be the last one." Obviously, they return to the habit. If you carry daily reminders that keep you focused on your mission you will be more likely to stay consistent with your game plan.

The transition of quitting smoking involves a few phases. First of all, identify yourself as a person who does not smoke, and amend your behavior accordingly. Consider what not smoking would mean to you in terms of benefiting your life. If you need to change your life schedules regarding how you spend time then do so. Also ask yourself about which hour of the day do you find yourself most vulnerable to give in to the temptation of having a smoke. Identify the reasons that compel you to do that during that time. Thinking about these things in advance will help you battle the temptation to smoke when these situations arise.

Positive thinking is another factor which will help you a lot in kicking the habit. With a positive frame of mind you can go a long way in aiding yourself in achieving your goals. If you can imagine yourself as a non-smoker and feel how good it would be; that alone will give you a lot of motivation to quit the habit.

Besides the specific given visualizations, opt for some relaxation techniques as well. These will help you to overcome your urges to some degree as they arise. They would also help you a lot in de-stressing yourself. You can do a search online for relaxation techniques and even consider what kind of techniques other people who have successfully quit smoking, have used. Based on your lifestyle, you can select one, or a combination of many methods that you can use to help you through your recovery. Also try to develop a habit of giving yourself a small treat on completion of each week when you haven't smoked. The same way that people on diets have "cheat-days" you should also reward your positive behavior for not smoking. On the contrary, if you find yourself slipping back into your habit, stop and re-focus. Don't make excuses, don't try to rationalize it, just stop, and get back on track.

Role of Will Power in Quitting Smoking

The saying "where there is a will, there is a way" is very relevant, especially if you are trying to quit smoking. The strong determination and will power you exhibit will help you in sailing through the roughest of weather. Cigarettes are very addictive as we all know, and the more you try to quit smoking, the more you'll find yourself drawn to them. Think of it like this. If you've been eating chocolate cake for the majority of your life and you decide one day that you will never take another slice again – you are going to find quitting very difficult. Smoking is a habit you picked up over the years, trying to leave it in a matter of weeks will be hard, but it is not impossible.

If you constantly think about how all your attempts to quit smoking in the past have failed, then you defeat yourself before you even begin. Many people laugh at the idea of positive affirmations – but they really do help. Twice a day, sit down and read off a sheet of paper phrases like "Today is another day that I am closer to getting my life back. I have decided to quit smoking not just for me, but also for the ones I love. I am happy, strong, and thankful that I have the willpower and support to leave this habit. Smoking was my choice, and now I am choosing to quit. Cigarettes will never have control over my life again, today I take control".

A lot of smokers all over the world have been able to get rid of the addiction to nicotine. Have you wondered how they have been able to get rid of this impossible task? There is no magical formula for this, but there are just a few steps which you can take for achieving your goal.

First, before you can change your life, you need to change your mind. Psychology has a lot to do with quitting smoking. You need to amend your attitude and feel that not smoking would do you a world of good. Keep in mind that quitting smoking requires a lot of work and there will be times when you want a quick fix. You need to be focused and strong at all times. The subconscious mind will always try to hinder your plan by bringing into light fictitious disadvantages of a non-smoking life, but that is the time where you need to be strong. Just focus on the positive aspects and the life which you would gift yourself with if you quit the habit of smoking.

To sum up, it's your determination and will power which will come to your aid while you draw up a plan to lead a smoking-free life. Medicine will help you with the physical cravings of puffing away, but to quit the habit for good, you need to be prepared to make changes mentally.

The Correlation Between Exercising and Quitting

There is a strong correlation between exercise in your attempt to quit smoking and actually succeeding. Smokers who exercise are revealed in a Gallup Poll to be twice as likely to quit smoking versus smokers who did not exercise. It has actually been confirmed through researches that smokers who take up a regular exercise program have obtained greater success rate in their objective to quit smoking. So the more you exercise, the higher your probability of succeeding.

For those smokers to whom cigarettes do alleviate stress, the stress level is likely to rise immediately after they quit smoking. But once you start to exercise your dependence on cigarettes for stress relief lessens since exercise itself relieves stress considerably.

The following list features a few of the benefits achieved through regular exercise:

Less Stress

More Stamina

Good health and well being

Fitness and Loss of excess weight

Toned muscles

Proper sleep

More energy

At the beginning select a couple of exercises that you would enjoy. It can be anything. Some choices are walking, jogging, biking, swimming, tennis, basketball, etc. You may even want to volunteer to do the strenuous yard work for your neighbors.

Unlike smoking, exercise is a good habit to pick up on. In your journey of a smoke-free life wouldn't you want to improve yourself in as many ways as possible? When you exercise, your body releases endorphins into your blood stream. Endorphins are your body's "pleasure" chemical and they help you deal with stress. Not only is exercising important for your general health, you may find it easier to quit smoking when you adapt to a workout regimen. To put the icing on the cake, your body will develop physically, talk about killing two birds with one stone.

Before you schedule your exercise program make sure to consult a doctor. It is advisable to exercise 30-45 minutes at a time, three to four times per week.

Never mind if you are out of shape, give yourself time to get in shape at your own pace.

A useful strategy is to consider exercising with a buddy. If you have a friend who is trying to quit smoking as well you will find it even easier to stay committed if they are going through the process with you. Having a friend or training buddy besides you makes exercising entertaining, and when you both make promises to each other, you will be more likely to keep them. Never underestimate the power of group-effort. The more people you can get to join your "stop-smoking" band-wagon, the more support you and your friends will give each other for quitting the habit for good.

The human body takes in a lot of toxic substances during respiration and during the consumption of foods and drinks. Again, due to the metabolic processes, different toxins are released in the body. The body constantly attempts to get rid of toxic substances. These toxins can harm the various systems in your body unless released on a continuous basis. Toxins can even be inhaled while breathing.

It's funny yet true that most of us do not breathe properly. We inhale oxygen with each breath. In turn oxygen is carried by the blood to every cell of the body. Each cell has got to receive a sufficient amount of oxygen to survive, remain healthy and provide energy to the body. Learning to breathe properly is also very important. Proper breathing can even cut down your urge to smoke.

First we have to make sure that we are breathing in unpolluted air. Since the air remains comparatively unpolluted early in the morning this is the best time for breathing exercises. Sit comfortably in a relaxed position without strain to any part of your body. You don't have to essentially close your eyes but it's my personal observation that breathing exercises work better with eyes closed.

Get ready, breathe in slowly and deeply. As you breathe in you will notice your stomach expanding as it fills with air like an inflating balloon. Let the fresh air fill up your lungs till its brim. Envision images of the air encircling the entire body. This image should give you a feel-good sensation. Then hold your breath for a few seconds and then very slowly exhale letting out all that foul air. As you exhale your stomach goes out like a deflating balloon. Also envision images of toxins being released from your body. Feel your body becoming a sanctified site freed from all the impurities that it had been carrying. After you have exhaled, pause for a couple of seconds, and again breathe in the unpolluted air peacefully to your heart's content. Make sure you aren't in a hurry. Repeat this exercise ten times.

Now it's time to graduate to the second part of breathing. Again sit with your eyes closed, but this time, keep one nostril closed with the help of your index finger.

Close your right nostril with your right index finger at first, and breathe in deeply through your left nostril. Hold the air for a couple of seconds, release your right nostril and exhale through it. It would be ideal to imagine images of clean air circulating though out your brain. Imagine as you exhale all the air that goes out is also carrying out all the harmful toxins from your body.

Repeat this exercise with the other nostril closed and in this way alternate between the nostrils at least ten times. Although this exercise shouldn't take more than ten minutes you will find that you feel relaxed and concentrated for moments afterwards. Practicing this little exercise for a bare three to four mornings would build in you the tendency to do the same whenever you get the urge to smoke. Also, doing these exercises as soon as you wake up, along with reading affirmations to yourself will prepare you mentally for the rest of your day. As you can probably imagine, this is a much better alternative to having your hourly puff.

How Jamming To Music Can Help You Stop Smoking

Music is a wonderful stress reliever. Listen to your favorite music at an hour you wish to light a cigarette. If you are at work and it's your lunchtime or coffee break, put on your headphones, switch on your iPod and stay tuned to music. It's pointless to suggest the type of music to listen to since taste varies between people. The only thing I would recommend is to listen to something that is soft and uplifting. Whenever you get the urge to smoke, your body is telling you that you need to relieve stress. Calm music usually has a therapeutic effect on your mood. The good thing about music is you aren't disturbing others. This means you can ease your tensions without bothering the people around you.

Meditate Your Way To Success

Meditation is one of the best methods to gain better control over you mind, body and spirit. Once you are able to gain control of your mind you can quite easily get over your addiction to smoking. You have to make sure you are meditating right for it to work effectively for you. Meditation isn't something you do once; you have to practice it regularly to notice its benefits. The more you meditate the more rewards you reap for practicing. This is an effective method but takes patience, persistence, and practice. Now let's digress a bit from our topic as I give you a few essential tips and advices on how to meditate.

In order to heal yourself through meditation you must realize its objective. The basic idea behind meditation is not to cut out all the forces around you but to become one with them. During meditation people are often found to detach themselves from the sight and sound of nature. Some even plug their ears with cotton to shut out sounds. This violates the very objective of meditation. On the contrary I recommend you to focus on the sounds around you. The simplest method of mediation that you could practice by yourself would be to sit in a very comfortable position with your eyes closed. As your mind drifts, meditation teaches you how to focus. Certainly this is a gradual process that improves with each practice.

First listen to the bigger sounds around you like the traffic .You can listen to even loud music from your neighbor's apartment. Then listen to the softer sounds like the drone of the refrigerator, or the air conditioner. Your focus should be to register in your eardrums gradually from the gross to the minutest of sounds around you. Finally bring your attention to the sound of your own breathing. You'll be able to do this after considerable practice. Meditation is about focus and having control over your body so once you are able to achieve this you will have much better control over fighting against your urges to smoke.

During meditation your eyes should be closed. You should try to visualize a picture in your head. Concentrate yourself on a self-conceived image; say that of a flame of a lighted candle or a single flower on a plant. Your challenge would be to keep yourself deeply focused and thoroughly concentrated on a single image for the maximum amount of time. It won't be easy in the beginning, the image will blur immediately only to be replaced by something else. Be patient and diligently work on it. Gradually you will be able to focus your mind on the same image for more than ten minutes.

Once you have reached this stage and have begun to practice it without fail, you know that you have reached your goal. This will boost your mental strength to gain control over your mind. This means the next time you get an urge to smoke, wherever you are, close your eyes and meditate. By the time you open your eyes not only will you find your urge driven away but yourself elevated as well.

How Acupuncture Can Help You to Quit Smoking

If you have tried all the methods in this book to quit smoking but found that they haven't worked for you then listen up. This is not a one method fixes all process. You need to apply the best method that works for *you*. Acupuncture may be the alternative you need that may help you quit smoking once and for all.

Acupuncture has started gaining popularity, for a wide variety of ailments and addictive behavior. With consistent treatments it is said to alleviate the urge to smoke. With acupuncture there is a success rate of between 85 to 90 percent in losing both physical cravings as well as the emotional need in relation to smoking.

One of the plus sides of acupuncture is that it can work against the problematic effects of nicotine withdrawal. It controls the nervous urges that patients have during their withdrawal period. The patient remains urge free until the next treatment. While doing acupuncture it is said that the appetite is not stimulated like other treatments so weight gain isn't a side effect.

How Does Acupuncture Work?

Acupuncture is the use of fine needles that are placed at various points thru out the body based off of areas called meridians. Acupuncture stimulates positive energy and dispels negative thru out the body. It doesn't give you any real pain (sometimes the needles pinch for a second) and can actually give a sense of tranquility and relaxation. After the acupuncture session the acupuncturist treats some parts on the outer ear. The patient's ear is taped on with an iron pellet that is designed to be used by the patient whenever he feels the desire to smoke. The patient squeezes the points on the taped ear and it aids in getting rid of the desire to having nicotine. Gradually the urge fades away with the smoking desire getting minimized as a result.

Endorphins come from the central nervous system and acupuncture has the power to rouse them. These natural opiates are 5,000 to 10,000 stronger as compared to morphine in order to give relief for stress. Normally it takes around five acupuncture treatments to put an end towards smoking.

The effects of acupuncture remain for quite a long time after treatment. You may think that sticking needles in your skin is foolish, maybe even juvenile but there are 47 diverse health conditions that are mentioned by The World Health organization that acupuncture can treat. Most importantly, nicotine addiction is on the list.

Some people even find acupuncture more effective then nicotine patches. The theory behind the nicotine patch is that you give your body smaller and smaller dosages of nicotine until you are able to wean yourself off of it. Acupuncture does not inject you with nicotine at all and in fact it can detoxify your body because your body gets rid of nicotine with the treatments. Also, since acupuncture stimulates your body to produce endorphins, not only will you be cleansing your body, but you will also feel *good.*

Acupuncture balances your nerves and gives you a sense of relaxation. In today's world, there is not a single day when we don't have tension, stress, and problems. These factors give birth to shallow breathing, quicker heart beats and digestion problems. Acupuncture can solve these problems giving you better health by alleviating bodily imbalances.

This chapter can be of paramount significance for you in aiding you to quit smoking. Acupuncture takes care of other health imbalances as well so you will be helping your body in more than one way without the use of chemicals or toxins found in other medication. Acupuncture is truly effective in helping you to quit smoking.

In accordance with the health experts, giving up the habit of smoking is truly of immense importance. Smoking gives you diseases like cancer of the lungs, bladder, mouth, larynx, pharynx, esophagus, pancreas, kidney uterus, and cervix. In fact, it also gives birth to emphysema and increases the chance of stroke by 30 percent.

Acupuncture not only deals with the factors that normally give birth to the habit of smoking but it also keeps your bodily functions in tune. So, acupuncture treatment can be incorporated in your treatment plan if you are planning to have a healthy body in general. This idea alone can boost your motivation. So, get started on quitting and forget that once you used to smoke. You cannot change the past but the *future* is always in your hands.

Quitting Cold Turkey

Quitting cold turkey is a method some addicts use to give up their substance of addiction. Cold Turkey means removing the substance without any substitutes. Cold Turkey is often the preferred method that smokers use to give up smoking. This is all about giving up the habit of smoking suddenly without any plan or thought about it before hand. In fact, people often presume that cold turkey cannot work without the aid of supplements like nicotine gum or patches because the withdrawal is so difficult.

My grandmother decided to quit smoking on the spot when one day she started gasping for air after taking a puff. Quitting cold turkey doesn't work for everyone, but if you feel strong-willed enough it may be the quickest route to ending your addiction. When you quit cold turkey, you throw away cigarettes and any objects that may remind you of it in one swoop. This means that ash trays, bongs, and lighters all need to go in one day. It's estimated that only 3-10% of people who try to quit cold turkey actually succeed, so it may not be the most effective solution for everyone. If you are going to quit cold turkey, you may find that using a nicotine replacement product may help you cope with withdrawal symptoms.

Quitting cold turkey is always the hardest, but if you can weather the storm, it's often the quickest method to ending your addiction.

Thomas Glynn (director of cancer science and trends at the American Cancer Society) suggests this method is tightrope-walking without a net. He believes the will of giving up smoking is sincere but the smoker generally does not factor in the severity of the withdrawal into the equation.

Why it's so hard to quit Cold Turkey

Cigarette addiction is physical and mental. For this reason, smokers often have to confront issues like irritability, insomnia, and depression after quitting on the spot. This mental withdrawal can last upward of three months to sometimes over a year.

Here are some things that can be done to help with the problems associated with quitting cold turkey.

Choose a time when you don't have as many pressures and responsibilities to go cold turkey. For example summer vacations or long holidays may work for you.

This tension free period may be just what you need as people generally smoke when under mental pressure.

Drink a lot of fluids. This aids your body to get hydrated and it is also something for your mouth to use as a substitute for cigarettes. This also helps your system to get rid of toxins quickly. Obviously try to avoid alcoholic drinks.

Stay clear of situations that cause stress and anxiety. Avoid places and functions where you know there will be smoking.

When the desire to smoke hits you close your eyes and count to 10 with some deep breathes immediately. You may find using a substitute (such as chewing gum and going for a jog) will help pass the cravings you get.

If you are quitting cold turkey you need to watch what you eat. Avoid excessively greasy food and don't consume any stimulants like caffeine or alcohol. These substances can interfere with normal bodily processes like the desire to sleep (which is actually really important when you are going through withdrawal).

During the process, you might forget the factors that prompted you to give up smoking so make a list of them and keep it with you.

Also, your friends and relatives should know about your situation in order to give you moral support.

Remember, one puff and you are back to ground zero. Find healthy alternatives that you can replace with smoking for when you get cravings (some people eat candy or chocolate, go for a jog or run, or even suck on straws or toothpicks).

To reinforce your decision and to make it permanent, you need to alter your frame of mind while you are trying to quit. Be aware of the negative impact of nicotine addiction, and know that it is not necessary for you. Make a conscious decision to understand that smoking is not an integral part of who you are. This will help start you to hate even the idea of smoking. Once these aspects are clarified in your mind, you can easily go with the cold turkey method.

How Laser Therapy Helps To Quit Smoking

Laser therapy is a relatively new treatment that has been found to be very effective in dealing with smoking problems. After conducting an array of tests on humans and lab animals scientists have decided to take this option public. Using lasers to halt a person's addictive nature is not a recent finding; the discovery was done in the early eighties and it was based on a fairly simple principle.

There are certain pressure points in our body, which correspond to key nerve receptors present underneath the skin. By applying pressure to these regions, one can trigger hormonal changes in his or her metabolic order. Most of the bad effects of cigarette smoking have to do with the interaction between nicotine and acetylcholine (a synaptic neurohormone). In order for this chemical interaction to reach and effectively bypass the nerve signals, applying pressure can bring about positive changes in the body. This underlying principle has been put to invaluable good use by acupuncturists, reflexologists and Shiatsu specialists, for a long time.

The method is fairly simple, a low intensity laser beam is applied on these regions and quite soon a chemical change is triggered which leads to a reduction in the number of cravings associated with the nicotine withdrawal phase. But just reducing the cravings aren't enough to beat off the cigarette smoking habit. You must undergo behavioral therapy to beat off the intense thought of reaching out for a cigarette every time you feel uneasy or just spaced out. This behavioral therapy helps you with whatever psychological problems you might face while trying to kick the habit.

This laser treatment is very simple and has practically no side effects. Do not worry, not all therapies mean that you'll lose your hair.

Laser therapy deals with nicotine addiction head-on so should you invest in it?

The choice is yours. Laser therapy technology is generally very expensive and investing in laser therapy means you are in for a huge financial bill. If you can afford the treatment, or if your insurance covers the therapy it may be the treatment method for you. If you are interested in going the laser therapy route but simply cannot afford it cheaper alternatives like acupuncture do exist and they prove to be just as effective.

Secondly just undergoing laser therapy for breaking your habit is not enough. Laser therapy will help beat your *physical* cravings for cigarettes, but your *psychological* problems will still exist – that is why it's important to follow up with a psycho-therapist as well – and no that does not make you crazy.

The Truth about Nicotine Patches

Are you thinking of investing in nicotine patches? These are relatively inexpensive tools to help you get over the nicotine withdrawal symptoms that pop up when you attempt to quit smoking. How does the nicotine patch function?

Well, it releases small amounts of nicotine into your blood stream. Whenever it detects a change in the body's chemical environment the nicotine is released and it thus beats your craving for cigarettes. You might argue that it does you more harm than good. Nicotine patches work similar to vaccinations in the body.

Remember with vaccines you are introducing a small amount of the living virus into your body. This encourages your immune system to synthesize its own anti bodies so that it can counter the disease when it later tries to enter your metabolic order in a much larger proportion. Nicotine patches can help you get off smoking by alleviating the withdrawal symptoms but you have to lower the dosage until eventually your body can do without it. It is recommended that you see a doctor and find an appropriate dosage before attempting to use nicotine patches or gums.

Another question you might find yourself asking is "how does one apply these patches to his or her body?" Well the technique is fairly simple. You can apply these patches to your upper arms, back or thigh but never on the same spot for more than once a week to get optimum results. Nicotine patches come in various quantities and are applied according to the stage of addiction from which the smoker suffers. A hardcore addict generally starts from a 21 mg package and later comes down to 14 mg and finally a 7 mg nicotine patch (whose application lasts for a period of 2 weeks) Even though nicotine patches are one of the safest methods of dealing with the cigarette smoking problem, they can't provide a fool- proof and final remedy for kicking the habit. This is because the intense craving for cigarettes can be triggered by watching friends smoke or staying in a place like a music studio which is generally stuffy due to smoke. Daily activities like having coffee can also trigger a cigarette crave if it's something that you use to do when lighting up previously. These social situations can and will probably provoke one to give into smoking so it's recommended that you avoid such instances throughout the period of your rehabilitation.

A quick fact to remember is that you do not need to wear a patch for 24 hours a day. Generally patches are worn when you first wake up and taken off at night (usually for 16 hours a day). Wearing a patch for longer than necessary will not help you kick your habit any faster and in fact may do more harm than good.

Before you give nicotine patches a try, discuss the options with your doctor.

Hypnosis Techniques

You can quit smoking undergoing different types of hypnosis techniques as well. Self hypnosis by watching some pictures or listening to something will help you beat the stress associated with leaving your smoking tendency. Secondly; you may even consult professional hypnotherapists and undergo one or more sessions in his presence which will help you to give up smoking as well. Keep in mind your budget while deciding which plan suits you the best. Self help sessions or face to face sessions with a professional hypnotherapist can be very expensive.

What Happens After You Quit Smoking?

The immediate rewards

About twelve hours after you have had your last cigarette, your body will start the process of healing itself. The level of nicotine and carbon monoxide in your body will come down, and that will greatly benefit your lungs and your heart, which were previously jeopardized when you were in the habit of smoking. After about a week or so, you will come across noticeable changes in your body. You may improve your sense of taste and smell as well. Your breathing will become easier, and though you may experience coughing, you will, in some time, be free of most of the harmful effects of smoking.

The immediate effects

As the body begins the process of self-repair, you may actually feel worse-off without smoking. Here it's important to remember that healing is a process which begins very soon but continues for a few weeks before reaching its destination. This is because as your body repairs you experience withdrawal physically and mentally. The recovery process is sure to be laden with recovery pains and withdrawal symptoms. As soon as some people quit smoking, they experience some recovery symptoms, like a short-term increase in weight which may be caused due to retention of fluids. Other such symptoms are hunger, tiredness, short-temper, temporary problem in sleeping and lot of coughing. These are caused due to the clearing of nicotine from the body, which takes about two to three days on average.

Long term benefits

It is very important to remember that the long-term effects of quitting are excellent. The sooner you quit smoking, the more you can reverse the damage that you have already done to your body. Of course short-term pains of quitting will arise but as we've mentioned multiple times it's important to stick with your game plan. After you quit smoking, you have a lot more days to live your life.

Most importantly, your risk for smoking related illnesses like cancer decrease substantially.

Fighting The Urge - How To Stay off for Good

Are you struggling to fight the urge to smoke? Here are some ways you can resist the temptation.

❑ **Remind yourself why you want to quit:** The majority of the battle of quitting lies within your mind. Though a lot of people find this difficult to believe, it is a fact. There is a reason why gum, nicotine patches and other replacement products have a success rate of under 10%, while hypnotherapy and other techniques are thrice as successful. It has become clear that quitting smoking is more related to your mind than anything else. Your conviction to stop smoking will benefit you more so then any technique discussed in this book. Remind yourself what particular reasons made you want to give up smoking in the first place. Think about the decision, and the people who are involved with it as well. If you give into the urge of smoking, you will let all of them down. Remember that like most of all, you have decided to quit due to the good effects it will have on your health, your life and also on people's lives who are close to you. Always keep reminding yourself about these facts.

❑ **Reward yourself**: Since the dawn of man, positive reinforcement gives strength to people to conquer tasks that they once deemed impossible. Set goals for yourself which you need to follow weekly, and reward yourself for achieving them. You don't have to be lavish, but even the smallest of favors can keep you motivated the most.

❑ **Have a backup plan:** You are going to have a few days where problems simply can't be ignored. Having a backup plan will come in handy in such a case. Having something to keep you distracted while you are withdrawing from cigarettes will prove helpful. For example, watching a movie with a significant other that wants you to stick with your goals can do wonders. Always carry a newspaper, radio, or game. These things can help keep your mind off of smoking when the cravings kick in.

❑ **Close support:** No comfort is better than a close friend being there for you during the difficult times. This makes you realize that you aren't alone, and that you haven't made a wrong decision. Your friends will constantly let you know that irrespective of what you might be feeling "for the moment", you have actually made the right decision.

☐ **Be involved in healthy activities:** Smokers find it easier to quit when they pick up a healthy lifestyle in addition to laying off the cigarettes. Exercising and proper nutrition not only will help you deal with withdrawal symptoms, it is good for your body in general. When you fuel your body with healthy food, your body will perform miracles for you. Some smokers find that drinking water with a straw allows them to have the same mouth connection as puffing on a cigarette. Combine your healthy habits with things that make your recovery process as easy as possible.

Expect the unexpected: Relapses

Though I am not suggesting that a relapse should be expected, the fact remains that about a third of the people who try to quit find relapses occurring. This normally happens during the initial three months of trying to quit smoking. If you experience a relapse, don't feel that something is wrong with your technique since it is very common to happen. Just because a relapse happened, don't allow it to overpower you. Just remind yourself that the position you are in currently is temporary – and that if you follow the plan that you create for yourself in as short as 30 days you will have a new you.

CONCLUSION

Some facts on tobacco before you finish reading

❑ Tobacco is the greatest cause of lung and oral cancer.

❑ Premature ejaculation and erectile dysfunction in men is normally caused by tobacco.

❑ If pregnant women continue to smoke, they can give birth to a diseased baby.

❑ A chance of a second heart attack looms large if a person who has had it once continues to smoke.

❑ Similarly, a second cancer can be in the making if cancer patients continue smoking.

❑ If parents smoke in their daily life, they will be spreading diseases to their children by keeping them in the vicinity of smoke.

Quitting depends entirely on whether you accept the consequences of smoking or not. The choice is yours. It's ultimately your life, and everything that has happened to it up until this very moment is a result of your choices. To live life by the cigarette is to live life in an ash-tray. George Bernard Shaw rightly said, A "cigarette is a roll of paper that has fire at one end and a fool at the other." You now have the knowledge and the techniques to quit smoking for good – so no more excuses – don't even think about having a "final puff". Start cleaning up your life at this very moment. Get your friends to support you, team work will always make coping with life's difficulties easier. Do what you need to do to stop smoking – no more excuses – no more procrastination, today is the day that you take action!

Printed by Libri Plureos GmbH in Hamburg,
Germany